D0211365

DISCARDED

Your body /
612 TUR

1001151

Turnbull, Stephan

Fraser Valley Elementary

Fraser, CO 80442 / 970-726-8035

Fraser Valley Elementary Media Center
125 Eastom Av. / PO Box 128

USBORNE BEGINNERS

Your Body

Stephanie Turnbull

Designed by Laura Parker and Michelle Lawrence

Illustrated by Adam Larkum

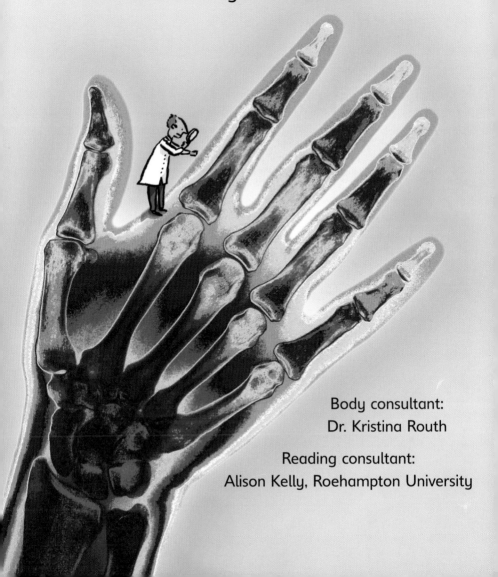

Body consultant:
Dr. Kristina Routh

Reading consultant:
Alison Kelly, Roehampton University

Contents

Man

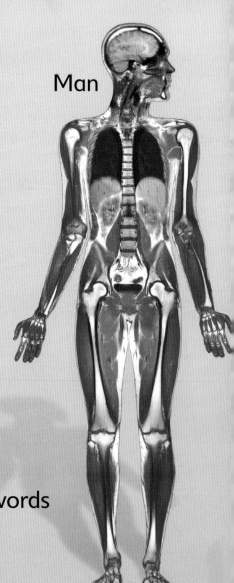

Your amazing body

Your body is like a complicated machine, always working to keep you alive.

Computer scans can show the different parts that make up a person's body.

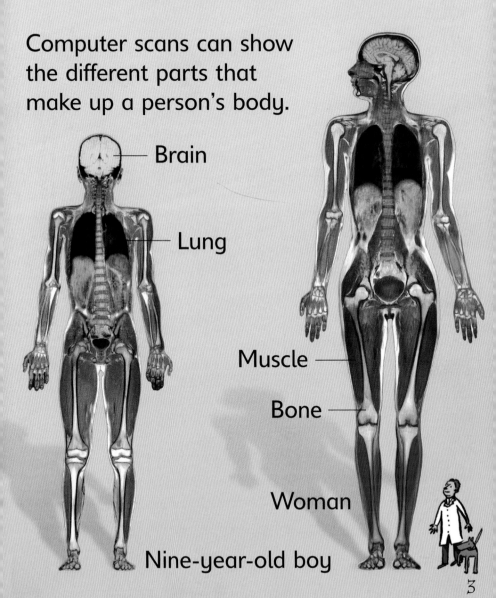

Brain

Lung

Muscle

Bone

Woman

Nine-year-old boy

Bony frame

Your skeleton is a frame
of bones that gives
your body shape and
covers its soft parts.

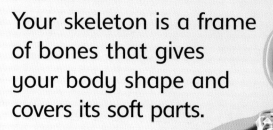

You were born
with about
300 bones.
Many of them
join together
as you grow.

Femur

Adults have 206 bones.
Femurs are the biggest bones.

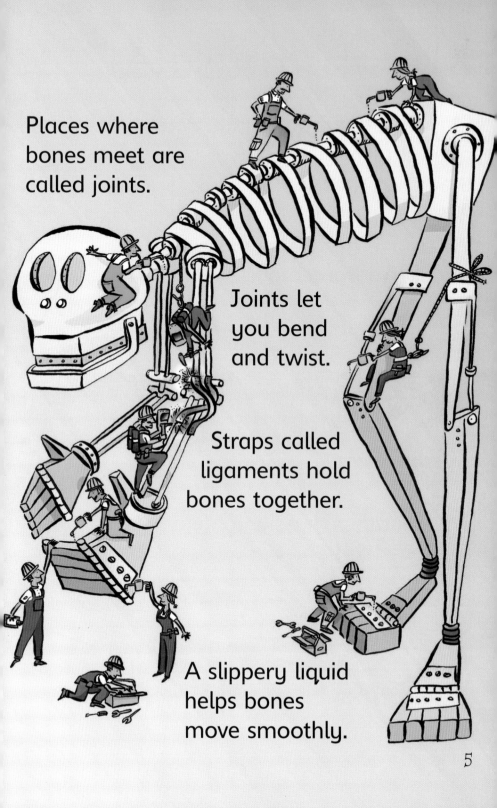

Places where
bones meet are
called joints.

Joints let
you bend
and twist.

Straps called
ligaments hold
bones together.

A slippery liquid
helps bones
move smoothly.

5

Mighty muscles

Muscles are rubbery and stretchy. They are often attached across two bones and help the bones move.

When one muscle tightens, it makes a bone move.

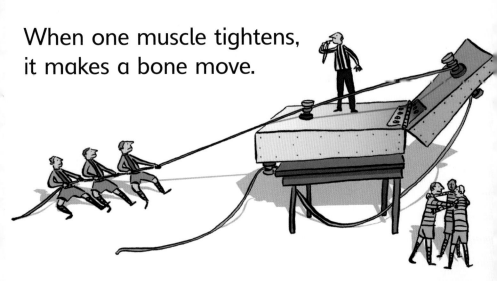

Then another muscle tightens to move the bone back.

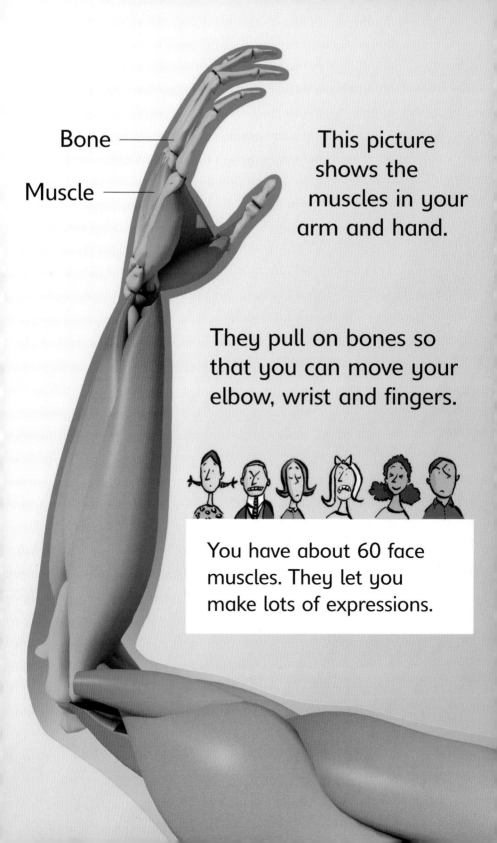

Bone

Muscle

This picture shows the muscles in your arm and hand.

They pull on bones so that you can move your elbow, wrist and fingers.

You have about 60 face muscles. They let you make lots of expressions.

Breathing

Your body needs a gas called oxygen from the air. You get oxygen by breathing air in through your nose and mouth.

Air goes down a tube called the windpipe.

Air fills two big, spongy bags inside you called lungs.

Then a muscle moves up and air is pushed out again.

8

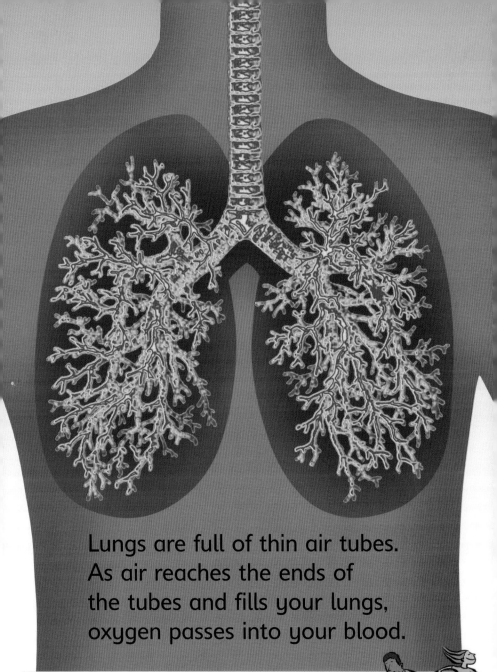

Lungs are full of thin air tubes.
As air reaches the ends of
the tubes and fills your lungs,
oxygen passes into your blood.

When you exercise, your body needs
more oxygen, so you breathe faster.

Powerful pump

Your heart is a big, strong muscle that pumps blood around your body.

Blood flows in and out of the heart through tubes.

The tubes go all over your body.

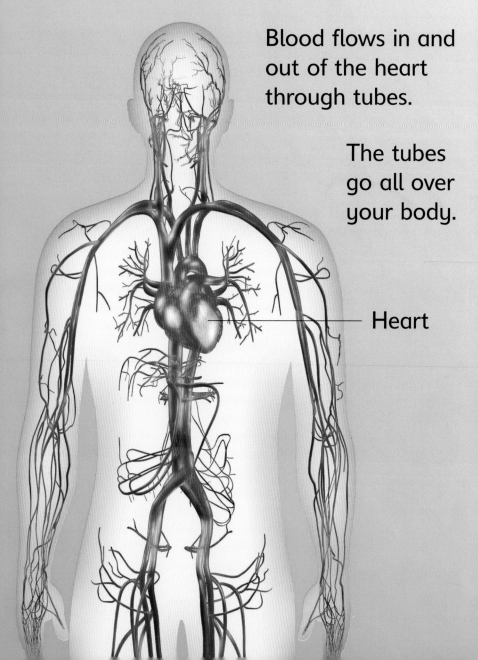

Heart

Blood flows into the heart. It is carrying oxygen that it collected from the lungs.

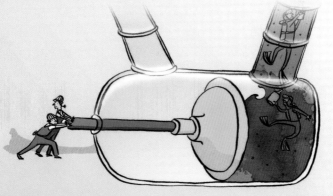

The heart pumps out the blood. This sends the blood rushing around the body.

The blood takes oxygen to every part of the body, then goes back to the heart.

Inside your head

Your brain takes up most of the space in your head. It controls everything in your body, and lets you think and learn.

The wrinkled, orange area in this photograph is a person's brain.

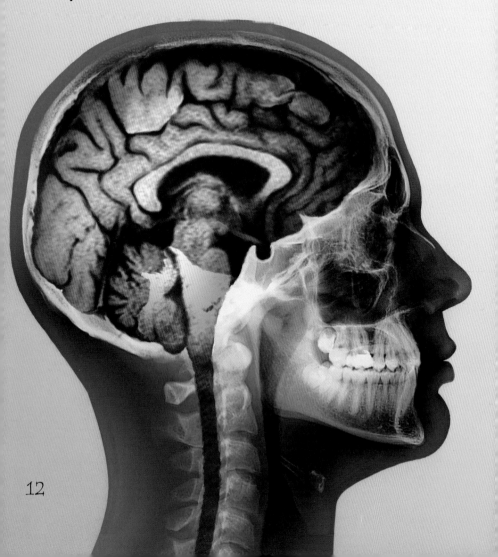

Here are a few
of the things that
your brain controls.

Smelling

Feeling hungry

Moving

Hearing

Learning and
remembering

Seeing

Dreams might be caused
by your brain sorting
out thoughts
while you sleep.

Passing messages

Your brain is connected to every part of your body by tiny threads called nerves.

Nerves pass messages to and from the brain.

This is what a nerve looks like.

It has feathery feelers that touch other nerves to pass messages.

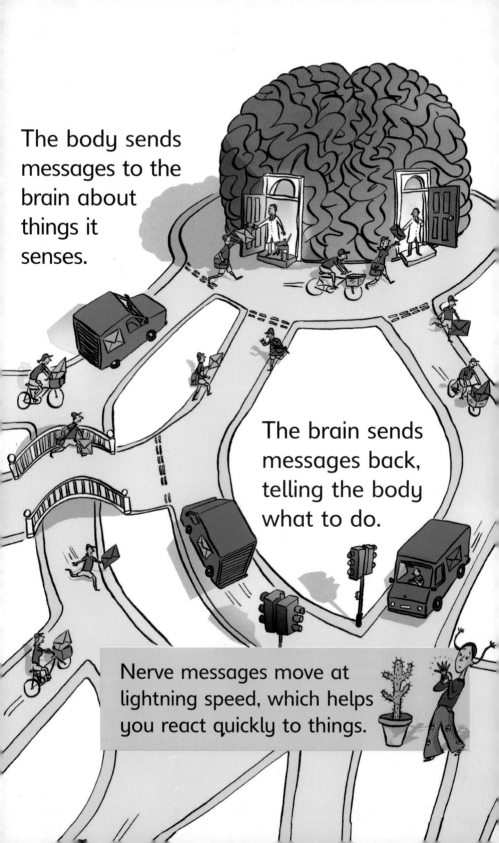

The body sends messages to the brain about things it senses.

The brain sends messages back, telling the body what to do.

Nerve messages move at lightning speed, which helps you react quickly to things.

Eyes and seeing

Eyes collect pictures of things around you then nerves send the pictures to the brain.

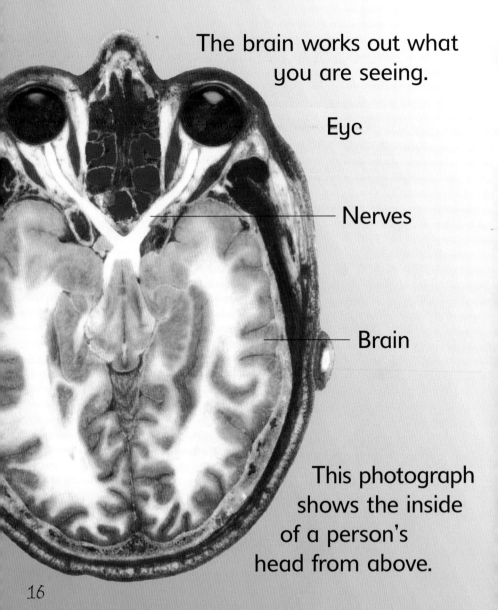

The brain works out what you are seeing.

Eye

Nerves

Brain

This photograph shows the inside of a person's head from above.

Light goes in
each eye through an
opening called the pupil.   Pupil

A thin layer of water keeps eyes clean so
that you can see clearly.

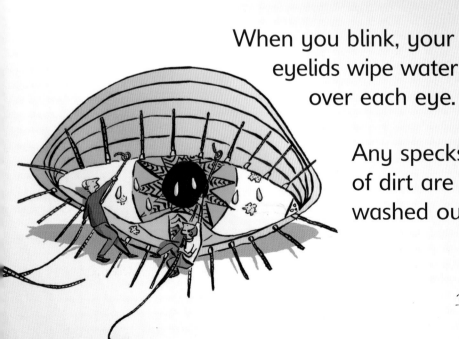

When you blink, your
eyelids wipe water
over each eye.

Any specks
of dirt are
washed out.

Ears and hearing

Ears go deep inside your head. The part you can see is a flap where sounds go in.

The ear flap collects sounds from the air.

1. Sounds go into your ear and reach a thin piece of skin called the eardrum.

2. Your eardrum starts to wobble, which makes three small bones shake.

Sound is measured in decibels.
The sound of a whisper is about 30 decibels. A plane taking off is 140 decibels.

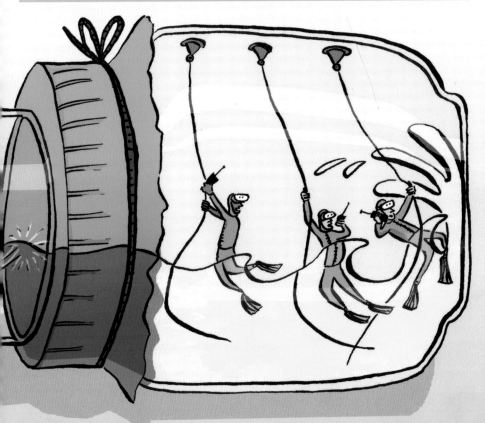

3. The shaking makes a liquid move deep in the ear. Hairs in the liquid sway.

4. Nerves in the hairs send messages about the sounds to the brain.

Munching machine

When you eat, your lips, teeth and tongue work together to break up food.

Teeth are covered in a hard coating called enamel.

They have roots that go deep into your gums.

———— Root

———— Tooth

Enamel is the hardest material in your body.

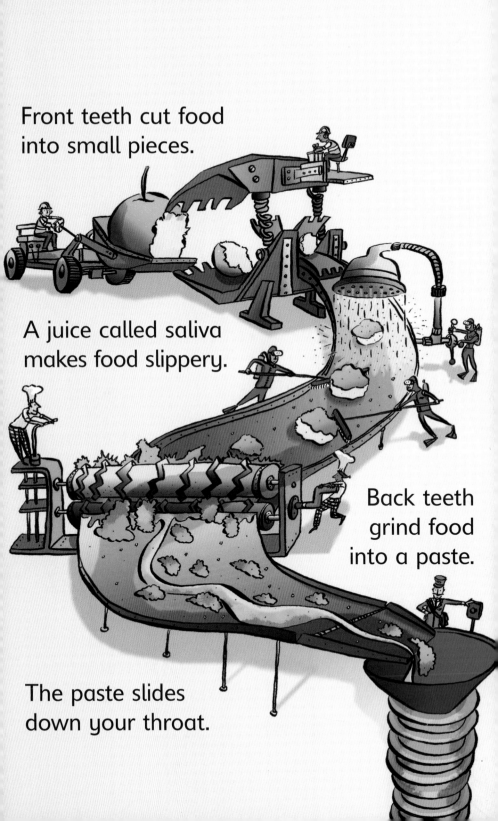

Front teeth cut food into small pieces.

A juice called saliva makes food slippery.

Back teeth grind food into a paste.

The paste slides down your throat.

Where food goes

Food that you have swallowed travels to your stomach.

Food is mixed in the stomach until it is a thick mush.

Next, it moves into a tube called the small intestine.

Special juices are added to break up the food even more.

Useful chemicals are taken around the body to give it energy.

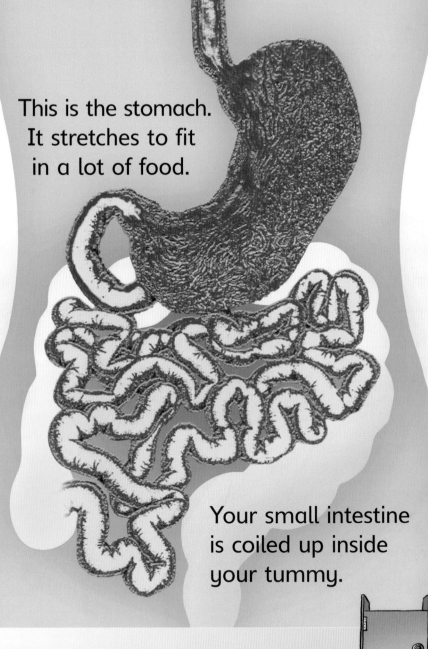

This is the stomach.
It stretches to fit
in a lot of food.

Your small intestine
is coiled up inside
your tummy.

Waste food is squeezed out of your
body when you use the toilet.

Water works

Your body needs to get rid of extra water that builds up in the blood. This job is done by your two kidneys.

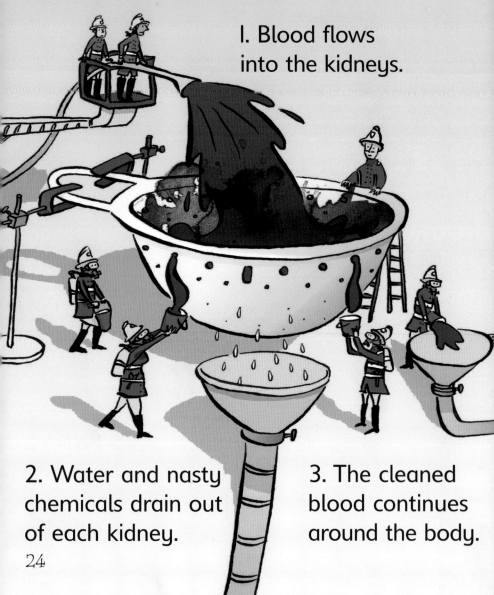

1. Blood flows into the kidneys.

2. Water and nasty chemicals drain out of each kidney.

3. The cleaned blood continues around the body.

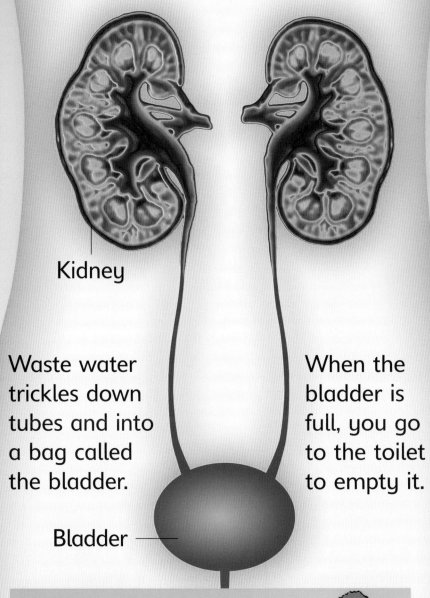

Kidney

Waste water trickles down tubes and into a bag called the bladder.

When the bladder is full, you go to the toilet to empty it.

Bladder

In just four minutes, all the blood in your body passes through your kidneys to be cleaned.

Outer covering

Skin holds your body together and gives you a waterproof covering. It is made up of layers.

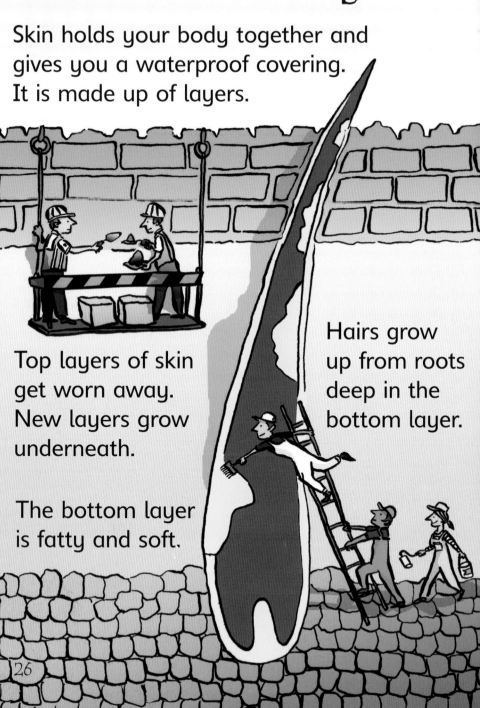

Top layers of skin get worn away. New layers grow underneath.

The bottom layer is fatty and soft.

Hairs grow up from roots deep in the bottom layer.

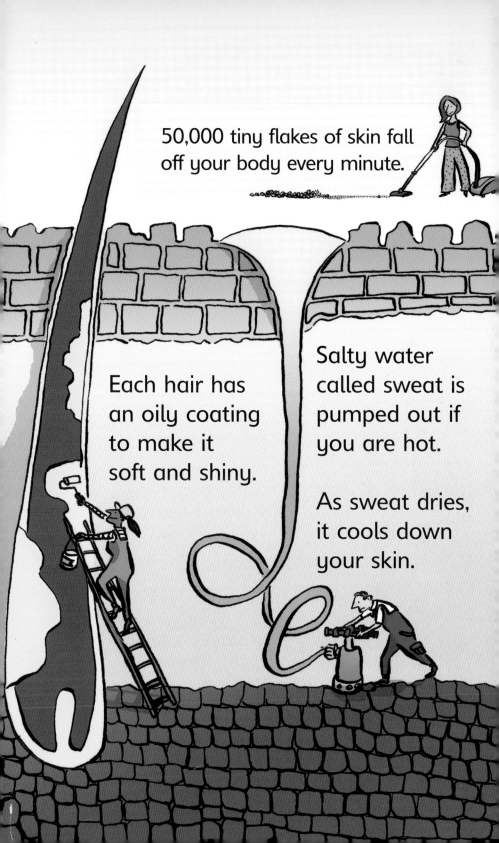

50,000 tiny flakes of skin fall off your body every minute.

Each hair has an oily coating to make it soft and shiny.

Salty water called sweat is pumped out if you are hot.

As sweat dries, it cools down your skin.

Under attack

Tiny harmful things called germs are always trying to invade your body.

Germs often get inside your body through cuts and scratches.

White blood cells in your blood find the germs and zap them with chemicals.

A doctor might give you medicine or pills that contain extra chemicals to fight germs.

28

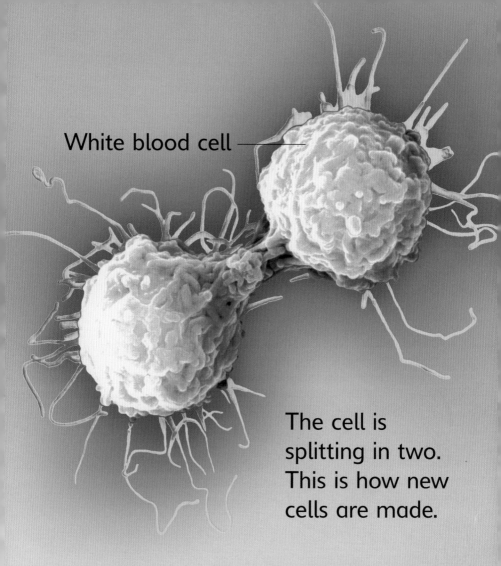

White blood cell

The cell is splitting in two. This is how new cells are made.

This is what white blood cells look like under a powerful microscope. Their long strands help them cling onto things.

If germs in your body are too strong to be killed, they can make you sick.

Glossary of body words

Here are some of the words in this book you might not know. This page tells you what they mean.

 ligament - A tough, stretchy band that holds two bones together.

 oxygen - An invisible gas in the air. Your body needs oxygen to work.

 saliva - Liquid in your mouth that makes food soft and easy to swallow.

 stomach - A strong, stretchy bag where food is turned into a mushy mixture.

 nerve - A thin thread that passes messages to and from your brain.

 germ - A tiny living thing that can get into your body and make you sick.

 white blood cell - A very small speck in your blood that fights germs.

Websites to visit

If you have a computer, you can find out more about your body on the Internet. On the Usborne Quicklinks website there are links to four fun websites.

Website 1 - Watch a movie about how your body works.

Website 2 - Decide where different body parts go in a game.

Website 3 - Find out more about bones.

Website 4 - Test how quickly your nerves and brain send messages.

To visit these websites, go to **www.usborne-quicklinks.com** and type the keywords "beginners body". Then click on the link for the website you want to visit. Before you use the Internet, look at the safety guidelines inside the back cover of this book and ask an adult to read them with you.

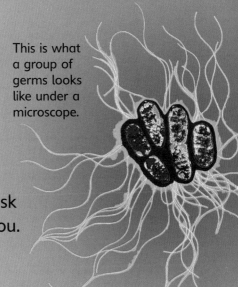

This is what a group of germs looks like under a microscope.

Index

Acknowledgements

Photographic manipulation by John Russell

Photo credits
The publishers are grateful to the following for permission to reproduce material:
© **Alamy** 7 (ImageDJ); © **Corbis** 1(Firefly Productions); © **Getty Images** 17 (Bob Elsdale);
© **Science Photo Library** 2-3 (Simon Fraser), 4, 9, 10, 23, 25, (Alfred Pasieka),
12 (Sovereign, ISM), 14 (Dr. Torsten Wittmann), 16 (Mehau Kulyk), 20 (D. Roberts),
29 (Stem Jems), 31 (Dr. Linda Stannard, UCT).

Every effort has been made to trace and acknowledge ownership of copyright. If any rights have
been omitted, the publishers offer to rectify this in any subsequent editions following notification.

First published in 2005 by Usborne Publishing Ltd., Usborne House, 83-85 Saffron Hill, London EC1N 8RT,
England. www.usborne.com Copyright © 2005 Usborne Publishing Ltd. The name Usborne and the
devices ♀♥ are Trade Marks of Usborne Publishing Ltd. All rights reserved. No part of this publication may
be reproduced, stored in a retrieval system, or transmitted in any form or by any means, electronic,
mechanical, photocopying, recording or otherwise without the prior permission of the publisher.
First published in America 2005. U.E. Printed in Belgium.